THE HISTORY DETECTIVE INVESTIGATES

VICTORIAN TRANSPORT

Colin Stott

HODDER
Wayland

an imprint of Hodder Children's Books

The History Detective series
Tudor Home
Tudor Medicine
Tudor Theatre
Tudor War
Victorian Crime
Victorian Factory
Victorian School
Victorian Transport

First published in Great Britain
in 2002 by Hodder Wayland,
an imprint of Hodder Children's Books
© Copyright 2002 Hodder Wayland

Hodder Children's Books
A division of Hodder Headline Limited
338 Euston Road, London NW1 3BH

Editor: Kay Barnham
Designer: Simon Borrough
Cartoon artwork: Richard Hook
Picture research: Shelley Noronha –
    Glass Onion Pictures

British Library Cataloguing in Publication Data

Stott, Colin
    The history detective investigates Victorian transport
    1. Transportation – Great Britain – History – 19th
    century –
    2. Great Britain – Social life and customs – 20th
    century
    I. Title II. Victorian transport
    388'.0941'09034

ISBN: 0 7502 3751 1

Printed in Hong Kong by Wing King Tong Co. Ltd.

Picture acknowledgements:
The publishers would like to thank the following for
permission to reproduce their pictures: Bridgeman Art
Library 4, 7 (top), 11 (bottom), 17 (bottom), 22 (top);
Hulton Getty 24 (bottom), 25; Mary Evans Picture
Library 6, 7 (bottom), 10, 11 (top), 13 (bottom), 15
(bottom), 19, 22 (bottom), 23, 24 (top), 28; Public
Record Office 27; Science & Society *cover* (Great
Eastern and Pullman Car), 1, 5, 8 (bottom), 9 (top), 13
(top), 15 (top), 18 (both), 19, 26, 27 (bottom), 29
(bottom); Wayland Picture Library *cover* (Broad Gauge,
Merryweather Engine and canal), 8, 9 (bottom), 12, 14,
16, 17 (top) 20 (both), 21, 29 (top).

CONTENTS

How did travel change in Victorian times?

Queen Victoria ruled Britain from 1837 until her death in 1901. Victorian Britain was one of the most powerful countries in the world, controlling a large empire abroad and leading the world in industry and trade. Victoria's reign also saw the arrival of many great ideas and inventions that have helped to shape the modern world.

The Victorian age was a time when life in Britain changed more dramatically than ever before. Among the most important changes were the great advances made in transportation. In 1837 travel was unreliable, expensive and slow – unless people were rich and adventurous they did not generally travel far beyond their local area. Farmers and manufacturers also had trouble transporting their goods around the country and tended to supply only the area nearby. However, by the time of Victoria's death in 1901, faster, cheaper and more reliable transport had arrived.

The history detective, Sherlock Bones, will help you to find clues and collect evidence about Victorian transport – so you can learn how people travelled and how this affected your local area.

Wherever you see one of Sherlock's paw-prints, like this, you will find a mystery to solve. The answers can all be found on pages 30 and 31.

DETECTIVE WORK

Visit your school or local reference library to find background information about Victoria and the Victorians. Ask your relatives if they have any old photographs taken during the Victorian age, especially those showing forms of transport.

Great Exhibition Catalogue, 1871

"If we had to sum up our age in a short phrase, it is 'the mechanical age'… There is no end to machinery. We fight with simple nature and, with our unbeatable engines, always win and prosper."

✿ How many different forms of transport can you see on this page?

WHAT WERE HORSES USED FOR?

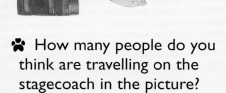

Despite advances in other forms of transport, horse power continued to be an essential part of the transport system throughout the Victorian period. Horses were useful in many different ways.

Wealthy people had their own horses and coaches. Most other people usually walked everywhere. However, on special occasions such as weddings, they might hire a coach for the day.

Before the spread of the railways, stagecoaches provided the main means of long-distance transport for people and post. Roadside inns provided fresh horses, food and accommodation for travellers, as well as selling tickets for the journey. Even though stagecoach travel was overcrowded and uncomfortable, tickets were expensive. Poor people could only afford to buy a ride on a carrier wagon.

✿ How many people do you think are travelling on the stagecoach in the picture?

Room for one more? An overcrowded stagecoach making a stop at an inn.

This water cart cleaned dirty roads by spraying water over them.

DETECTIVE WORK

Investigate the different ways in which horses were used in Victorian Britain. Libraries and museums will have information. You might also try local shops, breweries or haulage companies that were established in Victorian times.

Carrier wagons were mainly used to transport heavy goods. They were pulled by teams of horses and had wide wheels to stop them sinking into muddy roads. Carrier wagons travelled slowly along the bumpy roads. For this reason they were unsuitable for transporting fragile or perishable goods.

In cities, horse-drawn hackney carriages or hansom cabs provided a taxi service for wealthier customers – and horses were used to pull the first omnibuses. In towns and the country, horses and carts were widely used to make small local deliveries. Horses were also essential to farmers who used them to plough the fields and to transport crops and livestock to market.

Lady Charlotte Bonham Carter was a rich Victorian.

"…with all the horse traffic, there was an awful amount of dirt on the streets. Some of them were in a dreadful state."

Two cabmen waiting for a fare.

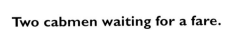

HOW WERE EARLY RIVER BOATS POWERED?

During the early 19th century, a lot of heavy goods were carried on Britain's inland waterways. Rivers had long been an important means of moving goods around Britain. Many parts of the country had their own specialised types of river boats. In East Anglia, there were barges with sails. These were called wherries and were used to transport farm goods such as grain and fertilizer.

Heavy goods were also transported along canals in specially designed barges and narrow boats. At first these were pulled along by horses. When a boat came to a tunnel there would usually be no path for the horse to walk along. Boatmen called 'leggers' would lie down on the boat and push it along by walking their feet along the tunnel walls. From the 1880s this job became less necessary as many canal boats were fitted with steam engines.

Locks on the Regent's Canal in London.

DETECTIVE WORK

With an adult, visit a local canal. Try to find out when it was built and what types of cargo were carried. Canals and bridges sometimes have construction dates on plates or carved into the stonework. Take rubbings of these to use as evidence.

Locks were built to allow boats to travel up and down hills. They were short sections of canal with gates and sliding gates at either end. Water was allowed to enter or leave the lock so that the water level rose or fell, taking the boat with it.

Canals were mainly built to link factories and mines to ports and large towns where goods could be sold or shipped abroad. Canal building had started at the end of the eighteenth century and by 1860 there were more than 3,000 km of canals in Britain. But by this time, it had become quicker and cheaper to move heavy goods on the railways – rivers and canals were no longer so popular.

A canal being built.

A Victorian wherry skipper's grandson later spoke of wherries:

"They had a square 'sal like a Viking ship in the middle of them and in those days they carried anything, people even, because it was the quickest way for people to get between Norwich and Yarmouth."

A Norfolk wherry.

❀ Wherries had a single mast that could be raised and lowered very quickly. Why do you think that this was important?

WHY WERE SAILING SHIPS IMPORTANT?

DETECTIVE WORK

What was life like on a Victorian ship? Find old books containing descriptions of sea voyages. If you have Victorian ancestors who emigrated to another country you could try to find out all about their experiences.

During Victoria's reign Britain led the world in manufacturing and trade. Much of this success was dependent on shipping. British ships carried raw materials and manufactured goods all over the world, and great ports such as London and Liverpool were booming centres of international trade.

These ports also provided a gateway for those emigrating to America, Australia and the far corners of the world. Some went in search of new opportunities while others went to escape from poverty. Many thousands of people fled from Ireland following terrible famines there. These emigrants endured long, uncomfortable and dangerous journeys before they reached their new homes.

❖ How do you think the two people in the picture on page 11 are feeling as they begin their journey to a new life overseas?

Look for clues to find out where the emigrants in this picture were travelling to.

Emigrants waiting at the dockside in Cork, Ireland, with all their possessions.

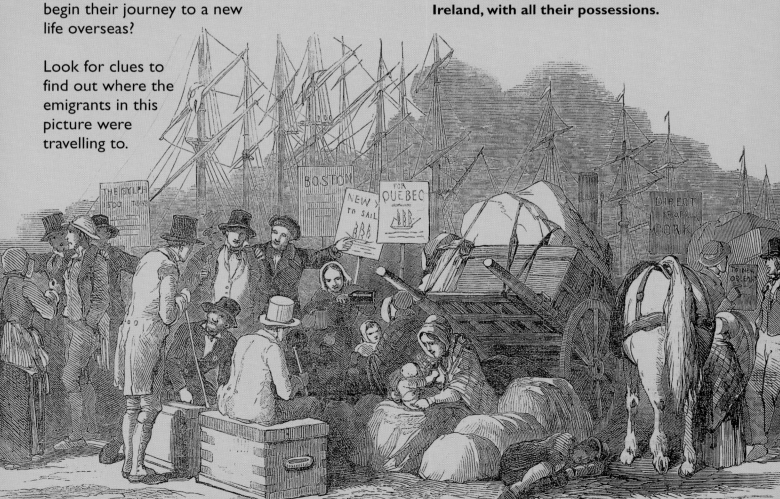

With the increasing movement of people and goods around the world, ships grew larger and larger. Ship designers began using iron to build the hulls of ships as it was much stronger and more watertight than wood. Above deck the bigger ships were a forest of masts, ropes and billowing sails. These needed large crews to maintain them.

Fast, sleek ships known as 'clippers' were built to take valuable and perishable goods, such as tea, quickly to market. At the start of the tea season the first ships to reach London with the new crop would get a very high price. Clippers would race each other at full speed all the way from China, in order to be the first in port.

The heyday of the clippers was short-lived as sail power gradually gave way to steam power on the seas. Sailing ships disappeared first on the faster cargo and passenger routes. However, they continued to provide the backbone of the world's shipping fleets until after the First World War.

Emigrants taking a last look at the English coast from the deck of a ship.

The flags flying on this clipper were used to send messages to other ships and to people watching from the land.

How fast were steam ships?

Steam ships had been in use before 1837, but it was only during the Victorian age that they developed into a practical form of transport. Early steam ships had sails that could be used if the engines broke down or ran out of coal. In 1838 the British ship *Sirius* became the first vessel to cross the Atlantic using only steam power. It took just 15 days to make the crossing that sailing ships would often take 40 days to complete.

At first, steam ships had large, wooden paddle wheels to drive them through the water. These were gradually replaced by metal propellers, which helped the ships to travel much faster.

An early Victorian steam-ship passenger spoke of the experience:

"The noise and vibration of the machinery was unpleasant, and to many people the smell of the steam was disagreeable."

The steam ship *British Queen* on her maiden voyage from London to New York.

DETECTIVE WORK

Steam ships caused great public interest. Look in your local Record Office for newspaper articles about steam ships such as the *Great Eastern*. You might also find adverts for shipping companies looking for passengers.

In 1845, the *Great Eastern* was launched amid great public excitement. At the time, this was the largest ship ever built. It could carry 4,000 passengers at the remarkable speed of 14 knots (26 kph). In 1866, it was used to lay the first-ever transatlantic telegraph cable between Britain and America.

Pioneering ships like the *Great Eastern* were good advertisements for British shipbuilding expertise – orders flooded in. By1897, British companies were building half of the world's ships every year.

As travel became easier and cheaper many Victorians took trips on river or coastal steamers. These pleasure trips were especially popular with people who could not afford to go away on longer holidays. Steam ferries soon appeared around Britain's shores.

The *Great Eastern.*

❀ Why do you think the *Great Eastern* was equipped with sails, paddle wheels and propellers?

❀ The distance between Liverpool and New York is 5,345 km. How long would it have taken the *Great Eastern* to travel this distance – travelling at top speed all the way?

Pleasure steamers on the Thames near Gravesend.

Was train travel expensive?

These third-class passengers were squashed into the London–Brighton train.

The rapid growth of the railways was probably the most dramatic and far-reaching transport development. It was viewed by the Victorians as a symbol of progress and innovation.

The first steam locomotive was built by Richard Trevithick in 1804, but it was not an immediate success. Heavy and unreliable, it kept breaking the rails that it ran on. However, by 1837 train design had improved greatly – Britain was now gripped by 'railway mania'.

At first train travel was basic, with passengers riding in open cattle trucks. But passenger comfort gradually improved. Coaches became enclosed – with heating and toilets! There were three classes of travel. The degree of luxury depended on what passengers could afford. Third-class travel was the least comfortable, but most popular, way to travel as tickets were cheap.

Poorer Victorians could now afford to travel. Many left their homes in search of seasonal or permanent work elsewhere. Others travelled for pleasure, with day trips and works excursions becoming popular. Seaside resorts developed around the country as more people began to take holidays away from home.

As transport improved, Victorians also had access to a much wider range of goods. Their diet improved too. Fresh foods could now be transported quickly from farms to towns – without going rotten.

DETECTIVE WORK

Visit a railway or transport museum to find out more about the development of the railways. Local enthusiast clubs may also have copies of advertisements for day trips and excursions that could be used to illustrate the growth of leisure travel.

A poster advertising special Christmas railway excursions.

❧ How do the people in this picture differ from those at a modern seaside resort?

Brighton was a busy Victorian seaside resort. Spot the bathing machines at the shoreline.

DID EVERYONE LIKE THE RAILWAYS?

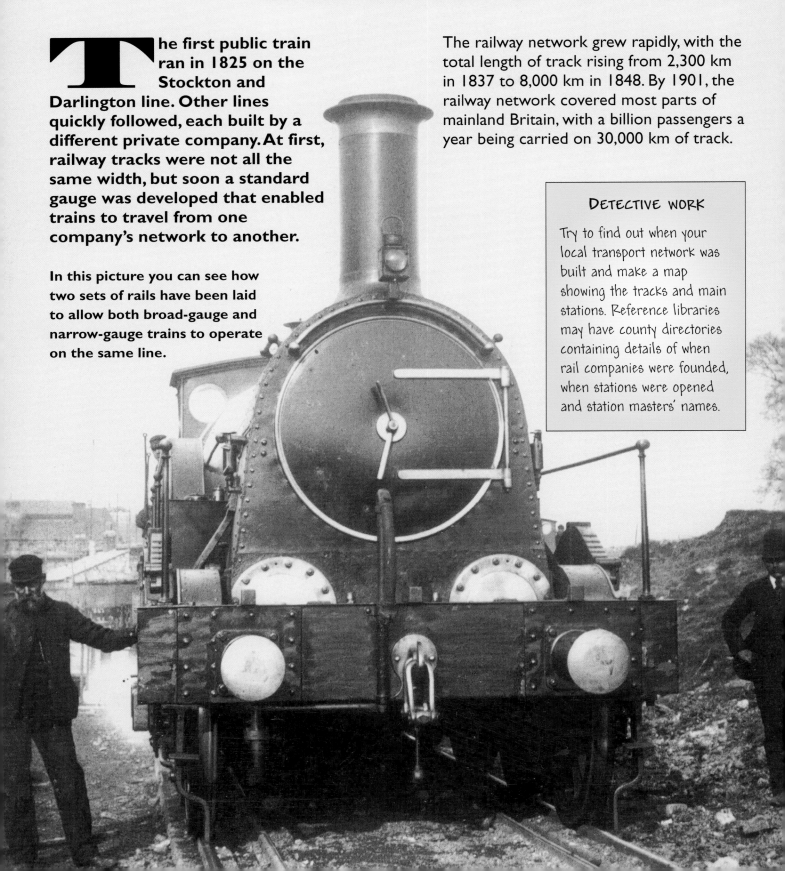

The first public train ran in 1825 on the Stockton and Darlington line. Other lines quickly followed, each built by a different private company. At first, railway tracks were not all the same width, but soon a standard gauge was developed that enabled trains to travel from one company's network to another.

In this picture you can see how two sets of rails have been laid to allow both broad-gauge and narrow-gauge trains to operate on the same line.

The railway network grew rapidly, with the total length of track rising from 2,300 km in 1837 to 8,000 km in 1848. By 1901, the railway network covered most parts of mainland Britain, with a billion passengers a year being carried on 30,000 km of track.

DETECTIVE WORK

Try to find out when your local transport network was built and make a map showing the tracks and main stations. Reference libraries may have county directories containing details of when rail companies were founded, when stations were opened and station masters' names.

The development of the railways had a dramatic impact on the environment. As the rails had to be kept as level as possible, tunnels, embankments, bridges and viaducts were constructed wherever the line met a natural obstruction. Stations, engine sheds, signal boxes and telegraph lines soon became features of the landscape.

Some people were not happy about these changes, fearing pollution and environmental damage. One critic complained: 'Between Slough and Wycombe the country is poisoned by the foulest, the blackest, and the most sulphurous pest of smoke'.

Most Victorians, however, were very proud of their railway network and the benefits that it brought them.

Floating the last span of the Royal Albert Bridge.

Bath station in Victorian times. The platforms are covered by wide arches made of iron and glass.

✿ Who do you think the bridge below was named after? What does this tell us about public attitudes to the royal family at this time?

WHAT DID ENGINEERS AND NAVVIES DO?

A portrait of Isambard Kingdom Brunel.

❧ What impression has the artist tried to give of Brunel?

The engineers who designed Britain's railways became national heroes. One of the most famous was Isambard Kingdom Brunel. He was a very imaginative and determined man who worked all hours planning and supervising every detail of his projects.

One of Brunel's most famous projects was the Great Western Railway, which ran from London to Bristol. He designed everything, from the track, bridges and tunnels to the railway buildings and carriages. Not content to stop there, Brunel even designed a steam ship, the *Great Western*, to carry passengers on to America.

But the unsung heroes of Britain's transport revolution were the navvies. Without the aid of machines, these labourers carved out cuttings and tunnels, and built towering embankments and bridges using shovels, pickaxes and gunpowder. Working this way, each navvy could shift an average of 20 tonnes of rubble per day.

The Clifton Suspension Bridge was designed by Brunel. It used a single span to cross the deep Avon gorge in Bristol.

19

The navvies worked in uncomfortable and dangerous conditions. Little regard was paid to safety. Men were frequently injured or killed in falls, railway cave-ins and explosions. On one line in the Pennines, 34 men were killed and 140 seriously injured while constructing a single, five-kilometre tunnel through the hills.

The navvies lived in filthy, overcrowded shacks built out of mud, rocks and scavenged bits of timber. In their spare time, their main occupations were drinking and fighting. Such riotous behaviour gained the navvies a bad reputation, so that, in contrast to the engineers, they were usually treated as villains rather than heroes.

Navvies constructing the main railway line from London to the North of England.

DETECTIVE WORK

Look for biographies of other famous engineers, such as Robert Stephenson and Joseph Locke, to include in your project. Record Offices may have copies of newspaper articles and government reports about navvies or accidents involving them.

In 1846 Thomas Carlyle, a Scottish historian, said:

"All the roads and lanes are overrun with drunken navvies… I have not in all my travels seen anything uglier than that mass of labourers."

HOW DID PEOPLE TRAVEL AROUND CITIES?

A horse-drawn tram.

Carriages called omnibuses were used to transport large numbers of people through city streets. At first, these early buses were pulled by teams of horses. Later, bigger and faster steam-powered versions were used in cities like Edinburgh and London.

'Omnibus' is a Latin word which means 'for all'. However, the fares were so expensive that not many people could afford to use them. Later, omnibuses became double-deckers with long benches fixed to the roofs. Poorer people squeezed together on these cheaper seats, where there was no protection from the weather. Many continued to use 'Shanks's pony' to travel about – their own legs!

In 1833, a journalist described what it was like to travel in a horse omnibus:

"Here we all are… six and twenty sweating citizens, jammed, crammed and squeezed into each other like so many peas in a pod…"

♣ How does the experience described above compare to rush-hour travel today?

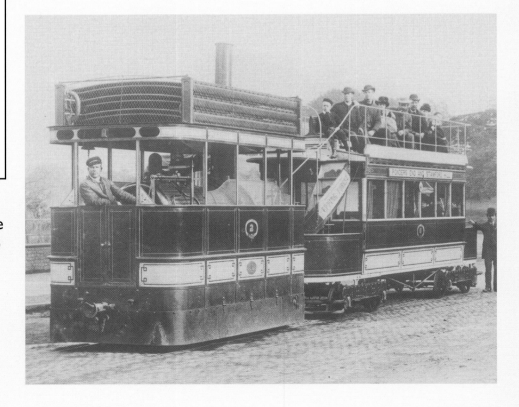

This tram is powered by a steam engine.

From the 1860s, trams were introduced into many cities. Early versions looked much the same as omnibuses except that they ran on rails. It was easier for horses to pull trams along rails than it was to pull buses along uneven streets. This meant that trams could carry twice as many people as buses using the same number of horses. And because costs were lower, tram companies could charge less.

Trams became very popular, especially when cut-price morning and evening tickets were introduced for people travelling to and from work. Trams became quicker and cleaner with the arrival of steam power in 1885 and electric power in 1901. Electric trams were seen as a very modern and stylish way to travel and they soon became the most heavily used form of city transport.

An electric tram rides through the middle of a busy Victorian street.

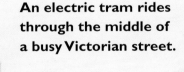

How old is underground travel?

Bigger cities, such as London and Glasgow, soon became more and more crowded with people and traffic. So, in 1863, the first underground railway was opened in London. It allowed passengers to avoid congestion on the streets above.

The first lines were built by private companies that wanted to connect a city's main railway stations, and to link these to the city centres. Early underground trains were pulled by steam locomotives and tunnels were filled with smoke and steam. Passengers had to carry their own candles or lamps to see in the dark! In the 1890s, electric trains with their own lighting came into use. Underground travel became a much cleaner and more pleasant experience.

A busy London street.

Underground tunnels being constructed near Lord's cricket ground in London.

❧ What sort of method is being used to construct the tunnels in the picture?

In 1896, a different method was used to move the trains on the new Glasgow Underground network. Fixed engines at the stations were connected to moving cables, which pulled the carriages along. When the driver wanted to stop, he would disconnect the train from the cable and apply the brakes. This system worked well, but the idea did not catch on elsewhere.

DETECTIVE WORK

Use modern and Victorian maps to illustrate the development of an underground railway system. You could show how houses were demolished and streets changed to make way for the Underground. Ask transport museums, Underground companies and Record Offices for copies of maps.

VIP passengers setting off on a tour of a new section of the London Underground.

In 1866, one London Underground traveller complained of:

"… *the darkness of the tunnels, the heat of the gas-lighted carriages in the summer, the sulphurous odour down in the stations, and the fear of unknown and indefinite dangers.*"

At first, Underground tunnels were built by digging a large trench, constructing the walls and roof, and then filling in the earth above. This 'cut-and-cover' process required the demolition of roads and buildings along the route. Engineers solved this problem by constructing large metal cylinders underground as they tunnelled through the earth. The new method quickly earned the Underground system its nickname of 'the tube'.

WHAT WAS A BONESHAKER?

A cartoon illustrating the perils of riding a hobby horse bicycle.

Cycling enthusiasts with their penny farthings.

Simple bicycles known as 'hobby horses' were invented before Victoria's reign. These were like scooters with seats. They had no pedals but were propelled along by the rider's feet.

The first pedal bicycle was invented in 1839 by Kirkpatrick Macmillan, a Scottish blacksmith. But cycling did not start to become popular until the arrival of the boneshaker in 1868, and the penny farthing or 'ordinary' bicycle in 1870. These bicycles were uncomfortable and difficult to ride, especially for women in long skirts.

A Victorian cycling club pamphlet from 1897 gave riders helpful advice:

"Never travel on a long journey without having your drawers lined smoothly and carefully with chamois leather or buckskin."

☙ Some Victorian men (and women too) thought that women cyclists were scandalous and wanted them banned. Why was this?

Women's fashion quickly adapted to the demands of the cycling craze.

DETECTIVE WORK

Make a cartoon strip illustrating the changing shape of bicycles during the Victorian era and beyond. Contact local cycle clubs. They may have information and pictures about cycling and cycling clubs in Victorian times.

In 1885, cycling really took off when the English inventor James Starley produced the first successful 'safety' bicycle. It had a light tubular frame, proper brakes, and a chain attached to the back wheel. Bicycles still follow this basic design. With the addition of inflatable tyres in 1888 bicycles became faster, more comfortable and easier to ride than earlier designs. Cheap to produce, they were soon in widespread use.

Cycling quickly became a craze and cycle clubs were formed all over the country. Members would get together at weekends for cycling tours and picnics. Races were also held using special racing bikes on purpose-built tracks. The sport became so popular that cycling contests were included in the first modern Olympic games in Greece in 1896.

But bicycles were not just used for fun. They provided poor Victorians with a cheap means of independent transport. Tradesmen with small businesses such as butchers could use them to make deliveries to their customers.

WERE EARLY CARS FASTER THAN HORSES?

A Benz motor car built in 1888.

🐾 Many early cars had three wheels. Why do you think that they became less popular than four-wheelers later on?

Automobiles first appeared towards the end of the nineteenth century and soon became known as 'horseless carriages'. This term was later shortened to 'cars'.

The first cars were cumbersome, steam-powered contraptions that were heavy and difficult to control. They improved greatly with the arrival of lighter petrol engines. The first car to be powered in this way went on sale to the public in 1885 – a three-wheeler built in Germany by Karl Benz. Inspired by the car's success, several British manufacturers developed similar designs of their own.

Early cars were very slow by today's standards, with a top speed well below that of a galloping horse! However, fears about safety meant that until 1896 motorists were forced by law to travel at walking pace behind a man carrying a red flag.

The Automobile Club was formed in 1897 to promote the new form of transport. But cars were not immediately popular. As well as being slow, early cars were noisy, dirty and unreliable. Passengers rode in the open, exposed to the wind and the rain, so they needed warm, waterproof clothes. Drivers wore goggles to keep the dust out of their eyes. As cars broke down a lot, most journeys involved a spell waiting by the roadside while the problem was fixed.

While they produced a great deal of public excitement, Victorian cars were too expensive for most people to buy. They remained a novelty toy for the rich and were not widely used until years after Victoria's death in 1901.

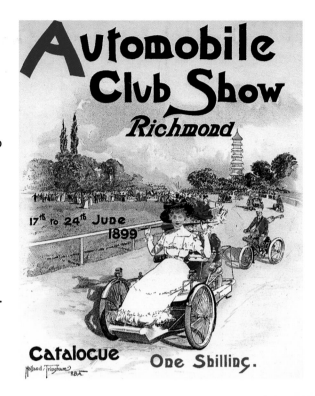

DETECTIVE WORK

Look in your local Record Office for newspaper articles on motoring in the 1890s. These may also contain adverts for cars and motoring organizations that can be used as evidence.

The Automobile Club's shows attracted a good deal of public curiosity.

These motoring enthusiasts are well protected against the weather.

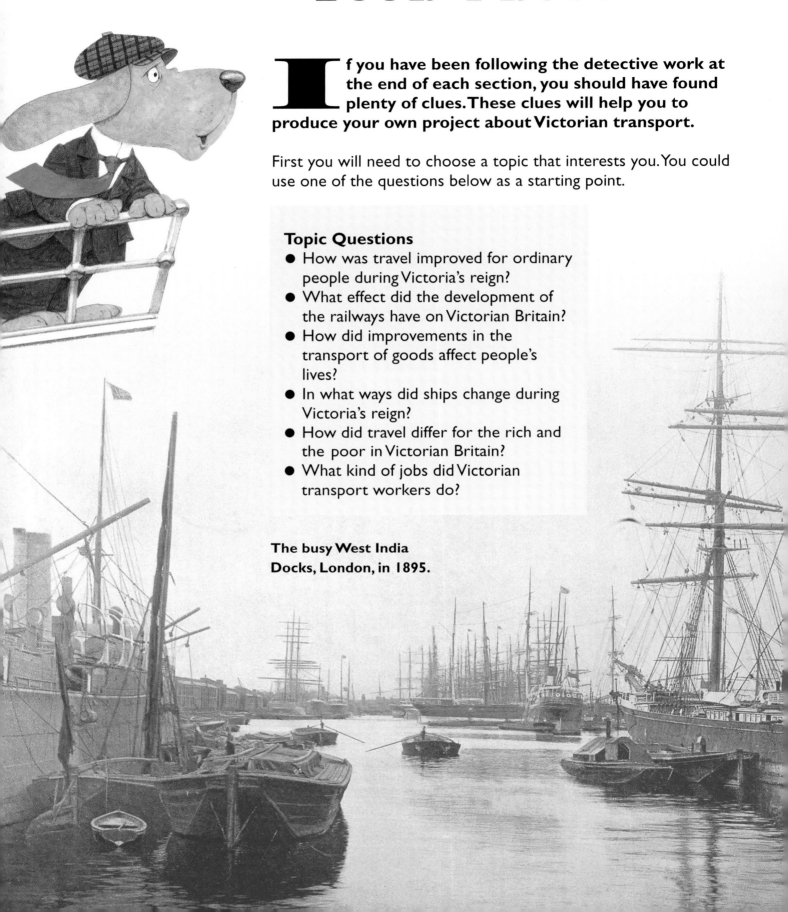

YOUR PROJECT

If you have been following the detective work at the end of each section, you should have found plenty of clues. These clues will help you to produce your own project about Victorian transport.

First you will need to choose a topic that interests you. You could use one of the questions below as a starting point.

Topic Questions
- How was travel improved for ordinary people during Victoria's reign?
- What effect did the development of the railways have on Victorian Britain?
- How did improvements in the transport of goods affect people's lives?
- In what ways did ships change during Victoria's reign?
- How did travel differ for the rich and the poor in Victorian Britain?
- What kind of jobs did Victorian transport workers do?

The busy West India Docks, London, in 1895.

When you have gathered all your information, present it in an interesting way. You might like to use one of the ideas below.

In 1892, the last broad-gauge train left Paddington Station, in London.

Project Presentation
- Write your project in the style of a Victorian's diary.
- Present your project in the form of a newspaper.
- Describe the journey of someone emigrating to America from a country village.
- Produce a brochure for a Victorian holiday company showing the benefits of the new forms of transport.

First-class train travel was very luxurious.

You might find an unusual subject for your topic. Sherlock Bones found that the development of the transport system made it possible to have a proper, national postal service. This helped people to organize their business and keep in touch with loved ones who had moved to different parts of the country or the world. This was very important before the invention of the telephone.

Glossary

automobile Another word for car.
barge A flat-bottomed boat used for moving goods on canals and rivers.
boneshaker An old bicycle with solid tyres.
canals Waterways that have been built by people.
cargo The things carried by a ship or boat.
construction The act of building. The word can also mean a building.
cutting A channel cut through high ground for a railway track.
embankment An earth or stone bank built to carry a railway track.
emigrant A person who goes to live in another country.
engineer Person who can design, build or maintain mechanical things.
gauge The distance between the rails of a railway track.
goggles Special glasses designed to protect the eyes from dust and dirt.
hull The main body of a ship.
hydraulic Operated by the pressure of a liquid such as oil or water.
lock Part of a canal that is closed off by gates so that the water level can be raised and lowered to let the boats pass through.
locomotive An engine for pulling trains along a track.
navvy A worker who dug canals and railways. It is short for navigator.
penny farthing An old bicycle with a large wheel at the front and a small wheel at the back.
port A place where ships can load and unload their cargo.
propeller A shaft with angled blades attached that is used to push a boat through the water.

Answers

Page 5: The picture contains three forms of transport – horse and cart, steam train and feet.

Page 6: Including drivers and those inside, there were probably about sixteen people travelling on the stagecoach in the picture.

Page 9: The masts of wherries needed to be quick and easy to lower because of the many low bridges over the waterways.

Page 10: They might be feeling scared, nervous and probably a little seasick.

Page 13: The *Great Eastern* was equipped with sails, paddle wheels and propellers because of worries over reliability.

Page 13: The *Great Eastern* would have taken 206 hours, or just under nine days, to travel from Liverpool to New York travelling at top speed all the way.

Page 15: The people pictured at the Victorian seaside are all wearing a lot more clothes than people would wear today. The Victorians did not approve of people revealing their bodies in public.

Page 17: The bridge was named after Queen Victoria's husband, Prince Albert. A large number of buildings and streets were also named after the royal couple. This suggests that the royal family was very important to the country.

Page 18: The artist has tried to make Brunel look noble and heroic. Navvies were not regarded in the same way.

Page 20: ❀ The experience of travelling in rush-hour traffic today is very similar to that in Victorian times. Improvements in transport have been matched by a rise in passenger numbers.

Page 22: ❀ The tunnels in the picture are being built using the 'cut-and-cover' method.

Page 25: ❀ In Victorian times women who took part in vigorous physical activity were seen as 'common' and 'unladylike'. There were also fears that it might harm their chances of having children.

Page 26: ❀ Four-wheeled cars were more stable than those with three wheels on rough roads and at higher speeds.

Useful Websites

London Transport Museum
http://www.ltmuseum.co.uk

National Maritime Museum
http://www.nmm.ac.uk

National Railway Museum
http://www.nmsi.ac.uk

School History
http://schoolhistory.co.uk

Books To Read

Canals – Building Amazing Structures by Chris Oxlade (Heinemann, 2000)

Victorian Railways by Andrew Langley (Heinemann, 1996)

Life in Victorian Times – Travel and Transport by Neil Morris (Belitha Press, 1999)

Life on a Victorian Steamship by Andrew Langley (Heinemann, 1997)

The Coming of the Railways by Pam Robson (Macdonald Young Books, 1996)

INDEX

Numbers in **bold** refer to pictures and captions.